Rumored Islands

Harbor Mountain Press, Inc., is a 501(c)(3) organization
dedicated to works of high literary merit. Harbor Mountain Press
books are distributed by Small Press Distribution, a non-profit
organization also, through GenPop Books and Distribution,
and through our website. The Press appreciates your support.

SERIES EDITOR
Peter Money

DESIGN
Edith Crocker

COVER DRAWING
Elizabeth Farnsworth

Harbor Mountain Press
PO Box 519
Brownsville, VT 05037

harbormountainpress.org

Rumored Islands

POEMS

BY ROBERT FARNSWORTH

Harbor Mountain Press
Brownsville, Vermont

I thank the editors of these periodicals, in which versions of these poems first appeared:

Antigonish Review (Canada): "Library"; *The Antioch Review:* "Cardinal"; *The Beloit Poetry Journal:* "After Dinner"; *Black Warrior Review:* "Realistic Satisfactions"; *Boulevard:* "Bricolage"; *Columbia:* "Petit Manan"; *Connecticut Review:* "Bright Thing"; *The Denver Quarterly:* "Eudaemonics"; *From The Fishouse Audio Archive:* "Vagrancy," "Winter Clock," "Fiction"; *Hudson Review:* "Eminent Domain," "Long Light"; *Innisfree Poetry Journal (online):* "Verge," "Mattering," "Nostalgia," "Sound Check"; *Malahat Review (Canada):* "In Contrivance," "Make Strange. Be True," "Referendum"; *Michigan Quarterly Review:* "The Sculpin"; *New England Review:* "Unforgivable Landscape"; *Off The Coast:* "Casque Bleu"; *Poetry & Audience (UK):* "Oracle"; *Poetry East:* "Why I've Never Bought You Fishnet Stockings"; *Smiths Knoll (UK):* "After Halloween"; *The Southern Review:* "An Eagle Finer Than Truth," "Wave," "Don't Start," "At Wendell's…"; *The Southeast Review:* "Yard Sale"; *Tar River Poetry:* "Snow"; *The Tampa Review:* "The Shutters"; *The Tennessee Review:* "The Maintenance of Awe"; *TriQuarterly:* "Emerging Figure"

"Yard Sale" also appeared in *Seeing The Blue Between*, an anthology of poems and letters to young writers edited by Paul B. Janeczko. "Fiction" was set by composer William Matthews (b. 1950) as part of a song cycle entitled "Ex Libris" (1997) for baritone & piano, dedicated to the memory of art patron Alice Swanson Esty, and received its first performance on 9/21/97. "Staircase" appeared in a festschrift volume for poet and translator Edwin Honig entitled *A Glass of Green Tea, With Honig* (1998). I am also grateful to the National Endowment for the Arts for a grant that supported the initial drafting of several of these poems, to The Frost Place, Franconia, NH, for the productive residency it gave me in the summer of 2006, and to Judith Robbins, the late Robert Branham, Beth Kanell, William Pope L., Sydney Lea, Cleopatra Mathis, and George Colt for their advice and steadfast encouragement.

Contents

For Georgia, Nathan, and Tobias

I

Oracle

for Tobias

Out in the huge careless
wind, my son runs past
the window, waving.

The leaves pause between
gusts, as if considering in
what form to return him,

and I recall the fluttering
inside that became edgy
laughter, when beside me

my father would begin
to draw. What's that?
You'll see. He would start

somewhere unlikely — an oval
of propeller, elk antlers,
a sloop's crescent combing,

some road dwindling off
into hills, a skater's scarf…
Perspective was his riddle —

those foreshortened curves
and vanishing points did not
describe things of this world,

but ways they meet the eye.
And go. As a pendulum
resolves — You'll see. You'll see.

Snow

The last sugary, shifty snow ceased by afternoon. Eleven
hours before the next, as yet most highly touted storm, the retired
bosun next block over is out behind his snow-blower in the dark,
straightening and polishing the right edges of his driveway.
Making ready. He likes to work in a parka and tennis shorts, his knees
bright red above a pair of clamboots. From time to time his Saigon wife
parts the kitchen curtains. When I straightened up with a shovelful this
afternoon, I felt the baffled fist of my heart close hard inside my ribs,
and I slowed down, but finished whittling a passage to the street.
Now he's out in the dark, at it again. We must belong to the pleasure
(for certainly it must be pleasure, even if that's just what duty has become)
that drives our flinging snow back into the dark it fell and will be falling from.
When he throws the whining tines into gear, I get up to make piano music
louder, glad to be lucky if not lovely in this life, but also irked by what
reflection reveals to me as fear. The shovel drips and drips from its hook
in my neat garage — what if the last thing I accomplished was its orderly
array of tools and toys? O the little inbred delights of inventing at once
disturbances and havens. So much depends upon the stupid, medieval
labors we continue. But it's *his* watch now, and I lean back in my
warm attic, I close my eyes and whirl up, whirl up in the arpeggios,
open them and look out across the illuminated quarter-acre pages,
pearled with lights, toward the storm forecast to find this coast by sunrise.

The Maintenance of Awe

for W. B. F.

When I was a boy and there was an hour
To kill, my father would take me to see
The world: a three-story pastel sphere,
Revolving gravely in its quiet courtyard.

Through an oak branching above the wall,
Just a glimpse of Labrador or Finland
Passing slowly through the leaves
Would stir me, and the shell blue oceans

Wheeling there in sunlight made my insides
Mutter and sing. Up close it was enormous.
Standing within its cool shadow, I would
Tremble under the ponderous azimuth,

Waiting for Tasmania or the Horn to appear.
There was a hatch in Antarctica so someone
Could climb inside to oil colossal gears.
Before the celestial order had become

Second nature, in childhood's Ptolemaic
Age, what little of the earth I knew
Seemed fixed and strange as the intricate
Designs on the Persian rug. But those blue

Longitudes gliding quietly over my head
Awakened buried certainties, curving, abstract
Intuitions kept like balance, that if made
Of any words could have only been flat fact.

Like the picture of an agate earth astronauts
Brought back so that we might be mystified
And humbled. Or this, father's recent snapshot
Of the world stripped to primer, Martian,

Blighted... no more the enthralling, legible
Sphere that memory has made into high, blue
Proof that life is larger (and stranger) than
Life, for having been imagined as the truth.

Eminent Domain

The house is already open as a stage set
to the sun. Awkward, almost gentle,
the excavator's scoop bites down
through the splintered second floor.
Plaster blizzards in the kitchen. A closet
door (with a porcelain knob!) dangles
from one hinge. Catastrophe doesn't
hold me here, nor the bitter thought
of someone's home bought just to be
demolished on a blue day in April,
nor even the sudden awareness watching
brings, of all the structures moviemakers
destroy to better represent destruction.
No, it's the performance, the stylish wag
and swing and grasp of that iron arm
that fascinates. How the bucket knocks
thoughtfully on a window frame until
it shatters, then digs intimately away
at the wreckage for a while. Stiff, polite,
it doesn't exactly mean to pry, even as
it's tearing out the wall. And yet despite
the man toggling inside its compound eye,
despite its repertoire of gestures, the machine
seems void of intention as gravity itself,
its leverings a clumsy adjunct to the wind
now shattering the tulips next door.
And a house with half a roof, an ancient sink
in bloom atop some rusty pipes, that awful
wallpaper; a house thus open to scrutiny
is hopeless, too inexact with overtone,
smothered in regret. Down with it.
Untraceable motive, terrible claw, down with it.

Nostalgia

for J. G. F.

Midnight alone. I could have made
my house my own with saxophones
or cellos, but hear those guitars?
They're still what gets me and they've
got to be loud, loud as these big
chords belled down the years. There!
There! They're how we'll be history,
how we'll be quaint, how we'll swing
ourselves up the long fish ladder
of middle age, how we'd like to believe
we might become someone's idea
of romance. How the blood can still
be blasted across provinces the careful
mind forgot, still know this pleasure that
makes that mind love its own defeat.
Once just some adrenal trigger maybe,
now they're how we'd hear the lost
(beside ourselves & baffled but
still thrilled) hopes in which we met
ourselves those years ago. Nobody
home, nobody wants me now, no
calls, no one to meet in the country
of old men, so I can crank it up and doze
here in the gale of guitars, mysterious
storms that love once strangely brewed
in my bloodstream. I can see them
lightning in the distance. I remember
how I followed them across state lines,
through all the bridges' narrowed eyes,
how in open cars we wore the brazen
chords like quicksilver breastplates.
Loud sun, loud rain poured all over me
and those I loved. Elders said you'll
use it up, use up all that devotional

passion, those verge-of-weeping smiles,
that sexual simmer — don't do it,
don't. I had to, as they did. And now
into the distances that music makes,
that music flings around my shoulders
like a cape whirling up in some old
wind, out of the here-take-this,
the won't-stay-done, the repose,
reprise, the run-around, out of my
sing-in-those-chains days I'm
sauntering with a smile. Listen
to those guitars. We were
as foolish and brave and certain as
anyone before us. What we knew
the young will never know.

An Eagle Finer Than Truth

In Memoriam A.K.H.

When many years ago something
I read said this was Keats: *Poetry*
is not so fine a thing as philosophy
for the same reason an eagle is not
so fine a thing as truth — no, I thought
no, not my man of loaded rifts,
of languorous last oozings, of carved
angels ever eager-eyed. So, he knew
all the body's failing, feverish needs,
so he yearned to follow the bird not
born for death — he had appetite,
and his sensational awe confirmed
my own. Now I can believe
his humility ran that deep, and no,
I suppose I cannot call the memory
his words bring back conclusive.
At twenty, I drove with two friends
around Cape Breton. There had been
a fire in a park we passed through,
and the road wound among granite
ledges and charred trunks, until it
suddenly gave on blank square miles
of slate blue North Atlantic... So
beautiful those cliff drops that the gut
plunged swiftly down until some
instinct gripped the wind, gliding
off into eastern twilight... I hadn't heard
from them in years, but until I found
last week the curt obituary, I liked
to believe that some of our reckless
joy survived. Now I'd just like this
to keep him there, beside a fire
down to coals, suddenly gusting
as our friend poured twelve-string

chords into the trees. Or between us
in that car, where turning a downhill
corner hard in waning light, we saw
wings unfurl across the windshield,
the tip feathers fingering an updraft —
finer, finer than any perfected inquiry,
finer than the fact of decades gone
and friends abandoned, finer still than
the truth of having fallen. In the downbeat
of those six-foot wings, we held our breath,
until he banked away across the water.

Seascape

Only after you've walked the furlong of hot
      sand toward its glistening does the sea

really enter the mind — a perception so vast
      it's already becoming idea, but locking

with cold your feet's sand-scoured bones, also
      massively and minutely resisting that transition.

All at once you are claimed: the sea's idea,
      until as ever, sensation starts composing its shadow,

its demurring echo — that heartening, creaturely belief
      that the soul won't someday lose but escape the body.

Mattering

Sometimes hearing new music,
the kind that thrills the triceps,
starts a cool cascade in the nape,
I wonder what if I'd heard this

back at twenty? Would my life have
turned, prompted by this beauty,
for good or ill, elsewhere? What if
then this something-like-a-door

had swung open inside of me?
But no, this melody could not have
existed then, at least not just this way,
and something in my body seems

fit for it only now. Now come May
I crank the skylights open, let
a slow freight's trundle pour in
on evening air, and spend uncertain

morning light replacing the world
with testimony. The exterminator
waves his brass wand gently along
the brick foundations of my neighbor's

house. A circular saw whines through
fresh lumber, behind doubled hammer
blows at work on a distant roof. More
efficiency, durability... And this more

comprehensively gorgeous music
I play again, again, avid for the taste
it gives of experienced, jubilant sorrow,
from which derives an old premise

even journalists would dismiss —
the world is growing, growing up;
a world that makes such music,
where every fervency of yes and no

admits a gentle irony, but where
honest admiration of the sky is still
required, that world must be growing
more complex, more aware. It isn't.

It is not. Suffering, pleasure, or
awareness of old suffering, old pleasure
simply come to seem more layered
and acute, like this changeable

spring sky. The floater in my left
eye veers across humid air that coils
from the street in a blast of sun, which
then diminuendos as the piano starts

battering the room with strange chords.
And if I know the simple hunger that
makes me confuse coincidence with
design, complexity with growth, music

makes me know, insists upon my
knowing. And insists as well,
tenderly, terribly, upon another
knowing, undulant in the distance.

Scion

Ghosts have a corresponding function to that of children.
— *Giorgio Agamben*

All that winter evening old friends
and my wife and I had been forgiving
ourselves our adolescent cruelties to adults,
solemnly supposing what was soon to come
with our own children now asleep upstairs.
When I walked the dog at last, under a smear
of January stars, a few ideas came, which seemed
to have the gravity of beliefs as they tumbled by,
flashing in the dark. Happy with their promise,
I whispered them visibly into the air.
Hours later, in my sleep, down a long hill,
through breeze-flung golden grass they came,
laughter sweet upon their lips, strange
and sweet as light is brief and immortal.
Their mirth was not concerned with me,
but I knew they would find me in a moment,
and from my thrilled and threatened distance
I knew them and ached for one cool drink
of their wise and innocent laughter. One in
Great War combat gear, puttees, and his rakish
little corporal's hat bearing a jewel, no, a tied
fly, and the other two arm in arm with him
in their era's leisure clothes, vest sweaters,
off-white ducks, saddle shoes. Ha! They
might have been golfers, and I the single ball
they'd played into the brief afternoon
of their foreshortened lives... I trembled in
the grass, waiting. When they found me
I knew they'd say so this is what you've
done with the youth we gave you, this?
And the durable yes I'd used to leech such
comfort out of my days would not suffice —

Yes, I've always said, *I do, I will, I'm on this, yes,*
giving all that mediocrity could, and more, to *yes.*
Yes? They would incredulously laugh, yes, this?
Well, we'll have to see then, we will have to see.
It's then I notice the blades of long leaf (iris?),
that with idle menace they draw across their palms,
and then the two civilians smile their almost
derisive, awful smiles, knowing I know what
terrible surgeries failed them. The soldier, trim,
spotless, victim of an invisible mortal wound,
again says we will have to see, and we do hope
you've passed it on to someone more inclined
and able, someone not so enthralled with comfort,
not so set on camouflage. And then they're past,
before I can hear if their renewed laughter
includes or disregards me, but it's the laughter
that gives me to know how sky and sea
and meadow just wanted gently into me to be
said back, and how with savage joy I will soon
be flung back into the wave's tilt and roil,
the thrust of leaf, the first faint wash of dawn cloud.
Then they are gone, and there is nothing
but the swath of their passage in the grass...

Bricolage

If I dropped the tiki made of varnished shells,
if it broke, there was no telling what misfortune
would surely, if not promptly, befall. Accidents

were not just emblems but triggers for the will
of everything to dust and salted ruin. Upstairs
in the twilight, as audience to mother's dozing,

Delphic after-baths, I came to understand that
motives only matter so much. Never mind
what might account for the tongue's sudden slip —

if that poinsettia, veering one day toward collapse,
then upleaving red and green hours after I douse it
should expire, there'll be no reconciling. If that

cloud, occluding the crescent moon to a threatening
tooth, lingers past a slow count of ten, no hope
survives. My subsequent chosen exile has turned out

haunted, homemade. I still know a ship requires eyes.
Some meat must burn to ash before each journey.
Manna, she explained, with covert smiles, is no

laughing matter — the bric-a-brac can see. A knock
releases the spirit of oak, and salt must never spill.
In a family, habits constitute culture — in our case

spirit-ridden, cross-purposeful with spells. So
many tripwires tuned like strings above the void.
I lived my life inside their melodies, until a figurine

of shells became an idol, worshipped like that minor
Guatemalan saint to whom I've been told the faithful
make offerings of whiskey and cigars. Oh, if the Moorish

arch of that wishbone were to topple from the sill...
If I mend the soapstone seal's broken tail, what
shall be forgiven me? What conclusion shall

I draw? Perhaps like my father, you have witnessed,
or you've suffered, some of the world's intricate pain.
He learned early how to navigate by stars,

and found his way to a shore piled with corpses.
I've not forgotten his laughter's thin neutrality,
when mother had discovered another fetish.

Now all these things were a kind of lover's joke,
something just between them. But if you don't
have ceremonies to complicate what custom

calls *because,* then how, on the fogbound coast
of awareness, where the forebears lead their perilous
afterlives, has your will survived without keepsakes —

flowers, shells, and bones — scrutable icons,
local stars, by which to read this earth and water,
between them forever polishing, and crushing?

Bright Thing

When they left the hedge shears
out overnight, I should have sat
my boys down with steel wool
and oil, and talked the metaphysics
of maintenance: greased chains,
cured skillets, putty & paint. But
like beliefs, satisfactions have
to happen to each of us, the way
this copper kettle became my spirit's
temple drum. Every June I spread
newsprint on the lawn, poured
polish into rags, and rubbed until it
made me squint, until it answered
daylight's fierce laughter on the bay.
My cousins did the brass: bed warmer,
hearth fender, andiron bulbs. When
we'd finished, the grass was strewn
with treasure. Beyond lost summers,
and the perishings to come, prepared
instruments blazed in the sun. Maybe
that's why I thought of its lid as
a rinsed but steady stone to balance on,
for climbing back upstream into the past.
Or I needed to keep hearing that lid's
creak and slam, as in winters when
it held kindling. Its ulterior fire was
my responsibility. So when it was
offered, I took the cauldron from
the old family house into my own.
It serves no use but catchall now,
but the boys have always known it.
As ever it tarnishes, obliging me, but
it's mine to invent a provenance for
— some colonial foremother, tending
a stew of lye and linen on the hob.

Next year they will polish it. And if
I don't explain, perhaps her revenant
might persuade them that life with
enduring things improves, braiding
ritual with use, with careful labor, with
the endless, elevated overhaul of clouds.

Cythera

Naushon Island, 2000

That at last I might share one of your childhood pleasures,
you led me down a forest path and out upon the bridge,
where salt-pond water now swung back through shadow —

swift, glossy, dimpled, black — and raced toward the sea.
Assembled there were a dozen people of all ages, most

to swim, all to admire the tide's cool torque, all in sunlight
picture-perfect: Eakins out of Watteau. And all, even
those about to leap and be carried away, turned an eye

to account for us, to ratify our belonging there. I made
a patrician smile my mask, and stuck close beside you,

remembering you, lithe-legged and wet-haired, in a picture
at sixteen, astride this bridge's rail. So my old wish
to have been yours was at last coming half-true — so much

water under this bridge. And what had all that been for —
why had all that beauty, that desire woken in me, survived,

if not to be recalled now, with humor-salted longing, if not
at last to let us savor this arrival? I looked the anointed
in the eye, then jumped with you and our various children

into the ebb to swim the half-mile home. And while we swam
I got to turning over in mind our walk through the woods,

the stories from your life now — of malcontented schemers
in Corrections. My evasive blather about failure, inertia.
Forgive, I thought, my remorses, maybe like those of inmates,

who can't own up to their situations, but nightly dream
scenarios very like this downstream swim, strange chapters

in their great escapes. A heron stepped slowly along the bank.
Eel grass slid by until woods gave way to meadow, and the huge,
shingled cottage appeared. Gnats turbaning above our heads

dispersed in sea-breeze. Of course I would remember this forever.
Of course. Cythera! Isle of beauty and pleasure. But I could not

get over how old we'd become, nor past this place, so long
one family's refuge — kept perfected as heaven's secret
from the rest of the century. Did just an ironclad trust save

this demesne from the usual greed, neglect, bad taste?
Why is it always less beauty now than who deserves

its balms that fascinates me? Your sidestroke calmly
turned to crawl as we neared the dock, your palms sliding
in with determined languor, as if beneath a pillow.

The kids all clambered out and headed to the house. When
we reached the warm planks, another life seemed almost

poised to appear from the ceremony you'd had us undertake.
But up on the sunlit slope, there was our improbably
extended family, waving us back from the irresistible tide.

Unforgivable Landscape

Near New Haven the landfills wear pathetic
green fringes beneath their gull-infested buttes,
where tiny yellow tractors crawl in a fine drizzle.
Above the junkyard leach ponds and the piles
of old tires, stare the incurable windows
of the valve factory. All those rusty coils, filthy
corners, ferrous mud — who'll say how we've
arrived at our nature? Rise or fall? Often on
this very road, we have wrangled into silences no
word seemed keen enough to rend, and couldn't
bring ourselves around to begin with our own
natures again, as with our hands and faces
and the weather we drive into... We're older —
now each struggle feels less dramatized, less
a matter under glass, more nature's matter-of-fact.
This nature we have made or acquiesced to,
which is no mere backdrop, but the whole of life
as it must be taken — going, going past, going
through us in the silences our arguments discover:
all the churning, suspicious steams from gun-
metal stacks, squat graffiti alphabets that
want to claim the mass of the wall or float up
like balloons. Gradually the commuter rails
vanish into copses, then small brown fields
the crows examine patiently on foot... Some
old roads still given to their original meanders.
And while neither of us turns, exactly, having
plumbed the silence, we do at last begin,
slowly, as after love, to talk more tenderly.

Cardinal

Which first — the sins, compass, prelate,
Or this bird? He seems more apt for some
Humid latitude, where the pale, sweet
Explosions of orchid light the dusk,
And macaws dagger their fuchsia tails
Among bromeliads. Here he must just

Be some kind of rubric. On a heaving limb
Of the birch he preens and pauses, crest
Feathers ruffling in a sharp April wind.
Oblivious icon, returned to be impaled
On the venerable myth — remember
That proto-finch, pierced by sacred nails?

I do still love how his name suggests
Its own dimensions, provides him camouflage.
This gray Wednesday the sight of him insists
That his stark scarlet originates the word.
Cardinal. Clinging to that raveled bandage
Of bark in a cardinal wind. Cardinal. The bird.

Verge

Next morning my son
comes customarily down
with his blanket, asks
for some of this hot coffee,
touches this shoulder
of mine with his scratched
hand. Strict sunlight slants
into the bag of maps
and tools I bent to gather
in the snowy clearing,
even as the canted tire
went on digging a trough
of icy mud, and the yellow
flasher, popped from its
socket, blinked. Snow,
pine sprigs, idling
breeze, pale green piles
of crushed window. Not
until I rise from my chair,
touch his nape with my
scratched finger, pour
his cup, and arrive before
the clock, am I here.
Saturday. Gently to wind
the old toothed wheel
back beneath its verge. Not
until I step with the dog
into sharp January air
do I discover three
emerald chips fallen into
my glove's warm finger,
and find myself regretting
how it fades: that wild,
barreling hurtle my
shoulders have, in honor,
in spite, been keeping like
the very secret all night.

II

Sound Check

Shape the mind so as to have it, among
the hours, repeatedly assailed, as if by
some demand imperfectly remembered,

and north light will say, Answer this,
after a long July day has sunk through
the refuge you've made of memory's

holdings: mismatched windows, a floor's
vague slope, furniture long since sold off
or burned, smells you wait, unaware,

to recognize again, answer this big tent's
evening air. Beneath the PA speakers
the drummer stamps his high hat,

tightens up the bass skin. The guitarist,
squinting as if peering into how it
should sound, twists a string toward E,

and the canvas walls belly in around
a hundred chatting voices. Imagine you
have to explain a flow of insinuations,

to descant for them a comprehension —
that child you saw today, staring
at herself in a hubcap, then, sudden,

strong, just as they all sling on their
instruments, the strained, beloved face
in the coffin arrives: no more, no more

evenings, chords, or clouds. She
was tired, tired of the brook's vague
laving of stones, emerald and nickel,

of all the vast, elaborate world's
complicity with itself. The music begins
its ravishing accusation of the dark.

The Shutters

A family who lived
upon a tidal islet,
beaded on a black

fingertip of fjord,
once included my life
in their own, open–

handed. Because
they had watched me
draw in the notebook

I kept, and felt for
my inarticulate need
to belong, they asked

me to paint, for their
sod-roofed mountain
cottage, a flower of

my own design upon
the shutters. It's too bad
about pity, the word,

how ugly it remains.
Whenever they called
me *clever,* I smiled

to think of the word's
inexplicable border
with *nefarious* in my

mind. They asked me
to paint the shutters.
And did I look around me,

though I had written
of the dwarf birches
in the upland pasture,

seeming to hold light,
even in the starless dark
I'd wait up to wander into?

No. No saxifrage or
heather informed my hand.
Thirty years I've known

how ugly my invention
was — an alien, stylized
result they must have over-

painted the next June —
it had nothing to do with
bone-strewn, glacial slopes,

with the frigid pond, with
boulders lichened blue
and burnt orange, with

tufts of succulent green,
nor until now with that
cow's huge, patient head,

suddenly filling the
window where I read.
The past should always be

this allusive gift. I did not
look around me. Even as
they wished me an ordinary,

happy life. Let this be then
a petal of homage, a grateful
prayer, indigenous and brief.

Wave

for Nathan

After a walk among the ferns and spruces,
after a fish hawk leaps up on a gust, after
the cliffside view of blue-black ocean, my son
tires and we leave, a strip of tall grass hissing

on the chassis. I liked those woods, he says.
You'll remember them, I say, some winter when
you're grown-up. A poet once said the child is
father of the man. Guy, he says, father of the guy.

I don't want to be a man. You're a guy. A man
looks down like a lamp. I don't laugh. Ok,
the guy, I say, I think you're right, that's better,
he's father of the guy. In minutes he's asleep.

The whole day's strange chord spells up in me.
My friend's tale of someone who'd played
a face game with her toddler, years later startled
when, looking up from supper, and pulling

the old silly face, her child said — *Hey mom,
remember this?* I drive out, past our house,
along the causeway, where this minute has
been waiting, all through the day's long skein

of sensations, watching me watch the copper coves,
dusky sleeves of pine, my son slumped beside me,
until it returns the wave that surprised us this
morning, after an hour of waves, suddenly cresting

the tide-ridge, frigid, foam-scrawled, whirling
away blanket, buckets, shoes — and I laughed,
until his dissonant whimper came to me, thrust
up like a needle through all the layers of light.

Library

Even if research can't account
for that old woman, crossing
herself as she leaves the bank,
even if the prime of things hides
under the waterfall's white adze,
or in the whirl of leaves across
a terrace, even if one can only
arrange the prompted deeds
of villains, heroes, inadequates
by results, not by motives —
still, within these walls we know
nothing is ever itself alone,
impervious, opaque. The worldly
eye resolves its cluttered depth
of field twenty times a second,
but here words must be divined
as back- or foreground, and every
figure is a tumbler of perspectives.
Waiting in this place, all
things chant their various lights.
Waves predicted for a thousand
miles brighten and break and
speak here. Hushed crosscurrents
flicker through clenched leaves.
How long this sturdy destination
has been taking quiet place!
Surely we were meant to dwell
forever in this house, this trove,
tool shed, cloud-chamber of
perpetuity. But we don't.
We come down from tall windows,
into the wind, released, as thoughts
to speak and be accomplished.

In Contrivance

the actual is at any
moment remaining
to be seen. Not exactly
waiting, not designed,
but under the breeze
remaining, as pale,
rain-beaded leaf backs
remain, as gold-
powdered pistils for
the bees' contriving
legs, as small, gristled
joints survive to hinge
our reasoning, hand-
to-head survivals.
Actual remains,
(don't ask — you know
the evidence is spring-
driven, self-perpetuating),
already instrumental,
through which becomings
blow like melodies
remembered, requiring
another instrument.
I thought my enumerating
praise was enough.
But now that I am walking
with a young, blindfolded
stranger on my arm,
across spring grass,
along the sidewalk, under
a sky that's deeper than
it has been for months;
I need to say the number
and nature of approaching
stairs. These circumstances

are somebody's contrivance,
of an afternoon, during
a first interview. How clever
he is, requiring us all to do
this, who had gathered,
as we thought, to take his
measure. Each passing
window bears a new
conjecture — *What's
the occasion? What's he
trying to prove?* I cannot
answer, only warn ahead,
tell what's there upcoming
in a soft, laughing voice,
leave silences for her
to experience muffled
light, earth, wind. So this
must be the narrator's
responsibility, contriving
passages through which hope
and belief will make their
surging, counter-currented
way. (All and only after
pretending, going along
with everything.) But there
remains what I will not
tell her. How small clouds
drag small shadows over us,
how, as if swinging free
of fact's dependable friction,
the crow sweeps through
those budding branches,
and how her hand's soft
grasp upon the inside of
my elbow is an agony
chaste and sweet and charged
with a dead woman's touch.

for Fred D'Aguiar

Long Light

Heading to work in a fine drizzle, after dropping
them at school, I watch a man in a silver hat lifted
in a bucket to the wires, to restore the dangerous

benefits of voltage. If my sons were here I might
explain him as hero, not perhaps with just that word —
but thinking about excess, about violent energies.

What was I roaring about? Shall I take this shame
to mean my anger was an excess of love? Why
did I twist their mornings so any thought of home

today will bring a hollow to their guts? I know
that hollow. Something in me seeks that loneliness,
perhaps to convert some long-dead pain to resolve.

Up there he's wrenching at a bolt, patiently but hard,
and down here my blood runs fresh and poisonous
at once, as if I had taken to heart at last something left

unfinished long ago. This current has no beginning.
It is theirs as well, a cold dream that will keep revisiting
each of them alone, to be survived. The steel arm is

lifting him down. Wiping rain from his face with a sleeve,
he hooks the wrench in his tool belt. The gloomy houses
re-inflate with light. The signal turns deliberately to green.

Realistic Satisfactions
(Or, Upon Westminster Bridge)

The difference between the sound of words in one age
and the sound of words in another is an instance of the
pressure of reality…
—*Wallace Stevens*

Earth had plenty to show more fair,
but the tour launches hadn't begun
guzzling upriver, and I was walking
in air already warm and rich with
exhaust, thinking *Open to the sky,*
open, open unto suburbs and the sky…
— strolling up from Chelsea, my head
full of lines a master claimed he wrote
atop a carriage on a bridge. I'd been
for several days a tourist, composing
a self in which collected novelties
might cohere: fabulous beer, strange
coins, looking right at curbs, the giant
Buddha settled beneath its temple
in Battersea, a calf muscle and five
grasping toes from the Elgin Marbles,
Blake's supernal blues and greens
cool in their gallery. Poetry, another
master once remarked, is a cemetery
of nobilities. But I had no urge
to honor nobility, just to loiter
in places that had moved someone
to words that had moved me. So I was
walking, casually, full of the melancholy
pleasure of being far away from home,
still safe in my own language, drifting
through places where every stone has
been re-laid in layers of words, down
streets that *have* been open to a sky

schooled with barrage balloons, pierced
with searchlights, suffering tortures
Wordsworth couldn't have imagined.
Oh yes, I knew the poem testified
to no fact, just to his capacity for vision,
for words to make the merely egotistical
sublime. But those fourteen lines had
survived, as surely as this city, and they
had *a calm so deep. The river glideth*
at his own sweet will... Feeling like one
who's just missed an irony's direction,
laughing nervously with or at myself,
I walked upstream, toward posterity's
little hoax, that sonnet's, this morning's
whence, the target bridge the Heinkels
sought, fixed beneath a torrent of traffic,
as a noble instance of clarity, the place
where all that mighty heart is lying, still.

Casque Bleu

So he must so he
stands up from within
outlandish leaves,
casts away the rifle,
tries on a smile he's
never felt his face
make before, and as
they approach gazes
down the valley of
the unpronounceable
river, whose stony
shallows, when he'd
scrambled to this refuge,
had quietly bickered
in the dark, and now
glitter furiously just
above the shoulder
of his captor, above
the vicious muzzle
of his gesticulating
gun. Sudden cloud-
crossed memories:
his daughter's sharp
voice, starlings routed
from an oak... How
warm the blue helmet
feels under his fingers,
as he stumbles down
this slope, dislodging
historical stones, up-
right in a posture
of excellent repose.

The Sculpin

"Marie, you get to call your teacher Marie?"
Dylan the fisherman's boy, incredulous.
"Well next year," he says, chewing hard
on gum my sons have shared with him,
"next year, you know, you'll have to call
your teacher Mrs. Something-or-other.
Whad'ya have, another stoogie?"
The little day-glo rod is parabolic. Nate
is excited, this first day fishing, and I say
"Knees on the pier, knees on the pier,"
doubting I'd survive a sudden plunge
in the Bay of Fundy. Even if
Dylan has been turning his lips blue,
diving from pilings on the patronizing
dares of smoking youths. Soon I'm hand-
lining up the ugly word, the little curse my
boys thrill to bring up over and over from
the bitter dark beside the pier. The sculpin
fights into the last foot of sun-struck sea,
struggles up behind the toothed coils of its
craw, flexing greasy pectoral fins, dangerous
dorsal spikes, mottled, puffing, outraged.
The mainland miles off is baking in the sun,
so the wind that comes to us is hot, suddenly
cool, then hot again. Dylan has a delicate
frame and face, a flute-toned, Welsh-tinged
voice. A gold earring glints under his red hair.
He and his New Jersey cousin are pleased
to demonstrate the gill grip one must use
unhooking sculpin. Then they drift off
toward the float, somebody's older brother
in a skiff. When I've rebaited my sons' lines
and advised them toward a fresh spot,
there's just time to savor the functional,
tangled beauty of spars and nets and winch

cables, over where the bright boats disgorge
their holds of pollock, hake, and herring.
They pour up by conveyor, into a fish house
attic where an old man wearing red suspenders
leans out into light. A drill whines where
someone's remounting a cleat. An ancient
diesel pump chimes. Mustard-colored,
scrotal strands of rockweed swirl like mops
in the tide swell. One scruffy gull keeps
shifting foot to foot atop a piling's copper cap.
There's a small commotion by the boys,
stomping, guffaws, then far off in the frigid
channel, finbacks come heaving up, slippery
and huge. My younger son, used to them now,
just tugs at my shorts and points. When they
blow, a sound comes like sheet metal beaten
with a mallet, a whisper with a gong inside of it.
So now there's mystery, distance, to complete
the picturesque particulars I've been trusting.
They've started up the bilge pump in that
red trawler. And now someone has hauled up
another stoogie, and I turn in time to see Dylan
brandish the ugly creature high above his head,
like Goliath's awful face, and with a snarling
laugh hurl it down on the concrete, hard.

Emerging Figure

Look. Within that eave-bound, up-under
attic light, that sepia behind November's
branches, up there, a man has been

recovering from his wife's forgiveness.
Stars smolder in that window's arc
of pale ceiling. He'd been just halfway

through regret's old waltz, wielding
the usual self-abasements, well-
stropped in two days of histrionic talk,

all to shape a future out of shame's
standstill. Now she has absolved him,
jump cut his ritual, and he doesn't know

where she's been, what door she opened
to kindness, and he can't decide between
the folly of searching recent scenes

for himself, lovable, and certainty that
her change of heart just arose somehow
from hours she lives beside him. Yes, I do

wonder why he deserves this evening of
voluptuous estrangement, that will veer
back at last toward miraculous connection

with the family of sleepers below. If
asked, I'd say he only ever plays
at loneliness. But no use exchanging my

envy for his pity. We have lives to live,
and to imagine. I am certain he can hear
the unstable octave of that single-engine

plane rise from behind this hill of darkened
windows, run the roof beam, fade. What could
it suggest to someone so swaddled in himself?

Tight life. Oh tight. I know. Nothing is
cast off there to be recovered. But when
he hears the crackling ice, the bottles

down here at the snow bank — me — then
he'll recall his evening's last, neglected
chore; slamming barrels down in crusted snow

below the window. Across the street, after
returnables, I'll be halfway down the block
before he lugs the first can out, but I know

he'll sing a little troubled air of thanks,
descending from his attic room to set things
straight, then sleep with a merciful woman.

Why I've Never Bought You Fishnet Stockings

for Georgia

Faintly chiming doors swung shut
on hissing traffic, and in the plush quiet:
mirrors: piles of bright cotton, pale silk,
frail hoops of beaten silver, sensible hats,
crazy shoes. Three clerks labored their
gum, as if beginning repeatedly to yawn.
Practiced at just looking here with you,
I knew where to find what I wanted,
but beside that display was a man
I'd have called overdressed, not exactly
settled into his long, well-tailored coat
and camel scarf. He was amusing a salesgirl
by spreading open a risqué pair of blue
silk panties at eye level, appraising, feigning
a feigned embarrassment. I left off paging
through a rack of garish skirts, and took
my glasses off, as always thus reassuring
myself I was indistinct as my surroundings.
Waiting for him to finish, I saw
a woman across the street step inside
a phone booth. Her slicker poised there,
a flame in a lamp. "I should decide," he said,
nudging giggles from the clerk, "she'll
catch up any minute." You know how
seconds of windshield wiping clarify not
just a movie hero's gaze but the fate he
drives toward? Well, staring through that
store window I began to wish that call
were stitching his life into a plot beyond
his grasp. Maybe the scarf, the cotton sheets,
a book would do as well to make your
birthday. My urge to get you the stockings

43

we had laughed about some years ago
was waning, and though the clerk had
already priced and bagged his small flirtation,
I was out the door, into the drizzle with my
self-regard, mumbling over the properties
of desire, when through the small rain
on my glasses, I saw her fold the phone
booth open, and stride away with a purpose.

Petit Manan

Though for the rocky verges I still have no
    good prayer, I've an ear for water music
in woods that spire across thin silver clouds.
    So near midnight I adjust the lamp to three
milk teeth of flame, and pick my way, past
    the maul I used to split half a cord this morning,
angled like a pump handle from a shining
    stump, down among the mossy harrows
of dead spruce, through the ferns, and out
    into the wind.
                 Half-tide waves, cold
and moonstruck, strive among the stones:
    endless, cruel evictions from what seems
eternity. For a while I listen to their chanting,
    until the visible circumference comes to focus
on the ledge beacon's pulse, certain as
    the sturdy soul's life in history, as what
in silent confidence the map describes
    of this ragged coast. Three flashes and a pause:
a little motive, a palmful of said beads,
    another tres divisa, to let us comprehend.
But our comprehending is impatient;
    it would be finished with or working up
whatever we've discerned, divided, dealt
    ourselves.
                 No wonder the indivisible
sublimely disregards us. I go back to
    admiring the speed of distant clouds, the sea's
demonstration of how the actual loves
    and suffers itself without beginning or end.
Tonight I would go on listening just
    for ways to praise this. I'd forego the axe's
ethical insistence, and trust a wakeful
    indolence to square my debts. Let me set off
as ever along the tide line, fixed
    by the moon's indifferent aim across the water.

Victim

When the shouts came we
were bent over salads on
the porch, bent on enjoying
lunch beside the pine-green
pond — when the shouts came,
urgent, anguished, inchoate,
when the kids began to say
they thought someone
must have gone under out
there, must be gone down
there, just across from where
that swimmer sat now,
under pines, head in hands,
no longer shouting, resignation's
cameo. And in the short reel
of anecdote this hour might
have become, the pedal boat
we frantically threshed across
that pond would be a farcical
streak of color. But there we
were. Ten minutes before
the rescue divers arrived
with their black rubber
equipment to shrink the pond
to one drop, I began
a myopic search: the water's
warm green-gold layer,
and then beneath it the chill
sepia of silted logs and weeds.
Fifth dive was the charm:
gristle-white, wavery, face-up
to the silver surface I rose
to beat and beat to show
the divers *here.* Here he was,
fifteen or so feet down,

beyond me, surely, and they
went down and heavily
hauled him up and onshore
beside his disconsolate buddy
kept on, kept on trying to start
the heart or clear the lungs,
as we pedaled absurdly back
to a float full of kids and parents.
As we approached, I flashed
on the memory of a pen, floating
there beside me, among my
dives, his? The only thing
I'd missed, emptying my pockets?
The fellow with me knew
without words that I'd have
nothing to tell, and he preceded
me up the path with gentle
headshakes. Nobody asked.
Until later, when the sheriff
required a statement. Even now,
years later, I can't exactly say
what's prompted this at last, unless
it is exactly what prevented
my telling the story to its distant
witnesses. Do I want to ward
him off or bring him back,
so long after he passed beyond
the water, the papers, into the earth —
after he's finally given up waiting
in my sleep for me, staring up
from the bottom at the vague
pane of sky, his stiff arms raised
like a child's from a crib?

Yard Sale

Gold-plate goblets freckled
with tarnish, disconsolate
pajamas, infant shoes, curling
irons, somebody's ancient

block flute, a candlestick grove,
bakelite coasters, egg poachers,
7 rubber sandals. Scruffy dolls
and accessories, board games

from whose battered boxes
children still look up with glee.
Two bald lamps, a basketball
and dumbbells, a toaster's chrome

full of early leaves, and tilted
like a grimy satellite inside
a crate, a two-stroke engine.
Now at last admitted to my

neighbor's back lawn, which
I've longed to cut across for years,
I see a tuft of grass and violets,
violets, growing, up in that

elm's clavicle, a little island
world in the air, where the trunk
divides. I wouldn't know how
to tell her of the delight I find

in this. But I think I'll buy that
small stack of teaspoons, just
so I can linger, picking up this
language, whose every word has

finally toppled over in one case
or tense or mood. Everything as is.

Referendum

for F.C.B.

Sunwashed haze brings up the ruined river's smell, slashed
with mown grass and diesel smoke. I get words in edgewise,
closing them inside storm doors. In one window a few still
waxy leaves, a romanesque wooden radio, doilies, a brackish

light upon the massy furniture. A note taped to a door handle
reads: *Gone to my Norma's for the day. Home this evening. Love, Claire.*
In her hand evening is an elegant word, already cool, promised
and replete. Some other starry time she'd known.

Down on the next floor's porch, a young woman narrows
her eyes in skeptical greeting. A flicker of breeze brings her
staggering smell, from across the table where she awaits the round
of beers a small, sallow elder woman swings between her knuckles,

laughing smoke, hipping the door open. Beyond them fresh
laundry is ranked upon tight staves. I smile at them. I have
information here, refutations of hysterical rumor, invitations
to consider every person whole and human, equal before the law.

But although my conviction, here it is just my information,
and I carry it up the dry rot stairs, slide it into door jambs, or
peevish hands, as foreign as if I had swung slowly down beneath
a parachute. I am wrapped in my genial refusal to explain,

to evangelize, which may be a form of respect or courtesy,
or maybe just refusal. In real, punishing light, the blaze
that makes the shade just dank, the venetian blinds the teeth
of the dust, and evening so coveted the bottles start tolling it

back by ten, I don't know about convincing. What is this dread,
for those the light cuts down, or for the stubborn valiance
some develop to survive, a tremendous effort surmounted
by a gilded plaster eagle, a crucifix, a flag? From the tenement

stairs I watch my friend covering the doors across the street.
She believes in reason, fervently and bravely, in gentle
victories of understanding. And the wiry old ladies who
captain the polls will rise early, resolved. The arrows must

be mended, the choices made in ink — this is how we say we
choose to live. But what secretly, surely breaks or sustains
us never makes its way in words. It listens to its own
breathing up here on the porches. It will not be pronounced.

Five more pamphlets. I feel like the boy up there, on that
pizzeria roof, slowly climbing a ladder set against a blind,
white wall. Into a random scrimmage of capital letters he
brings a bright red comma, cradled like a football on his arm.

Zethus, Wandering

for Arthur & Marianne Whitman

It seems an age since the night I asked my brother
If he thought music were meant to shelter or expose us,
Forever since he glanced back with what looked like wonder
In the lamplight. That is the face that I uncover

In my dreams now, ten years since our great house
Burned to ruin, since Niobe's wailing rage rose
Above the bodies of her children. My nieces and nephews.
Olive boughs rake the stars in groves where I drowse

The nights away as I began, an orphaned recluse,
Wanderer of lethal memories, awful dreams.
We were kings, I and my brother Amphion, whose
Ecstatic lyre assembled the cold stones, and composed

The walls of Thebes. I was there, though it seems
The tale thrives without a witness, maybe the part
Of his life the solid surviving stones redeem
In their survival. Behind my sledge's straining team

I watched the boulders we'd had faced for ramparts
Tremble and convene, as he struck and strummed and bent
Those seven strings. And laughed for a joy no human heart
Should know, perhaps, laughed madly in a transport

Of blazing comprehension. Every chord, blent
Anew by the three Lydian strings, pulled a slab along
The slope and into place, and left the sharp scent
Of crushed thyme in the summer wind...

After that, I believed my brother, believed in the strong
Device the god had made for him, of a turtle's shell
And the antlers of a stag. My fingers stumbled among
Those strings, but his could raise the stones with a song.

Together we fashioned seven marble gates in those walls,
And ruled the growing city without quarrel many years.
Niobe bore him seven sons and seven daughters, all
Strong and handsome, and in our magnificent halls

There was always singing — lyre, pipes, kithara cheered
Our palace nights, and in that sounding air our city thrived.
I listened, I believed, I loved, I put away the spear
For husbandry and music. Flushed with wine, we'd engineer

Imaginary temples, whose dimensions derived
From the intervals Amphion played in torchlight.
Every colonnade or tower, arch or pediment we contrived
Miraculously rose from his hands upon that prized

Instrument: a city made of music and of moonlight.
It was not the god's pure and simple fire that graced
Those seven strings — I will not believe that. Delight,
It was, delight beyond divine understanding, — a site

Of pure beginning. Whenever the music took place
It found its image within us already, vibrant. Each
Imagined phrase and echo seemed to wait
Like a universe of crystal to declare itself, to be amazed

Into being in the air. Even now, I believe...
Niobe meant nothing but that she was happy, proud,
Yes, too proud. But I would damn these gods, these
Jealous, childish gods who'd erase us just to please

Some vanity! Out here, in my rags and tattered shroud,
Beyond the limits of my stolen, gleaming city, where I
Live now as weather and my poor neighbors allow,
I care nothing for their edicts, their endless, loud

Demands for loyalty and love and sacrifice.
Let them save themselves. They will have to sing us
Back from the changing clouds one day. Thebe and I
And our infant son survived the massacre. Why?

They know. But would my knowing make our Itylus's
Fall end in other than his death? Then Thebe fell.
And I took up this wandering. Nothing but those
Sufferings, and the letters of our names will survive of us,

Of the house his music built. The lyre vanished — shell,
Strings, yoke — smashed and scattered with my brother's bones
Beneath the heavy earth. Not even these seven-gated walls
Will last forever, but music, which could not save us, will.

Don't Start

Over the phone, through which we struggled
so clumsily those many years ago, I now try
to describe the process of loading the camera.

But I haven't the vocabulary to convey the steps,
which aren't difficult, just (for a decade's worth
of my having done them by touch) inarticulable.

And we almost tumble back into something like
those old set-tos, but save ourselves. The boys
are asleep in the suite's next room after a long day

sightseeing, and neither of us could bear having
bickered at such a distance. Yet we used to bear it
somehow, didn't we, remember? Now because

I know it's coming, I'm charmed by the rehearsal
of your aversion to cameras. You keep fumbling
the leader into place across the tiny room behind

the shutter, and while I ask if you can feel little
cogs through the bordering perforations, I am
thinking of our wild cousin-in-law, who calls

monthly for commiserating sighs to punctuate
her own ventilations of pain, and how you
hand me the phone with a *good luck* look that

maybe says you've forgotten those anguished toll
call silences between us twenty years ago. Now
I'm judging the progress of the fire I've read beside

all evening, and then you divine somehow,
perhaps in a faintly anxious mid-sentence quaver,
my intention to be off soon, to leave the house

for some hours (the theater and a beer) —
you hear my intention to be gone, you hear.
And in your voice I hear, with an exquisite quarter

swoop of spirit, I hear your consequent shift
in tone, a certain cool flatness there, even as I
also hear the camera click shut and the auto-winder

whir. But we don't start, as once we might have,
no — I say where I am going, and you where you
are off to with the boys and the camera tomorrow,

and you yawn goodbye, until Sunday at the airport.
For better or for worse (and it's thrilling not to
know which), we don't, as once we might have, start.

III

Thanksgiving

for Georgia

A magnificent gale blew
         all night on the northwest
wall by our bed — gusts

         I loved to picture raking
empty oaks. I'd woken to
         your warm haunch beneath

my hand, and waited, as I
         would have thirty years ago,
for a shutter to break loose

         and batter shingles. In
half-sleep, then half-
         recalling the old shutters

long since stacked
         in the cellar, I watched
moonlight rinse your face,

         then rose to the window:
swift sketch of meadow —
         cedars flung, and waves split

white beneath the buoy's
         plunging star — crux of a wild
zodiac, in whose distances

         I'd always imagined my love and my tasks.

After Halloween

Now the leaves are
down, autumn air
exacts half a mile,
and off on a little rise
to the north, beside
the fresh white siding
of her house, a woman
pins laundry to a line.
Above, her gable's
half-moon window
uncannily returns
the stare of my own,
for which, it seems,
up attic this first
November morning, I
am the skeptical spirit.
Three shirts struggle
on the breeze, then
a sheet, inspired
as a studdingsail. She
vanishes behind it.
No more than she
might step off a yardarm,
off the foot of this page,
into the air you are
breathing, shall I be
released from this life.

Écriture of Habit

Just when I began to suppose I'd something
maybe significant to write, I began to want
to paint. Simple scenes: light gladdening
the stones, the water, trees — just the staunch
quidditas of things rendered as they are.
I'd long ago done vanishing points, and bowls
and cones and fruit; it would be second nature.
No. Facing the desolate filigree, I couldn't unfold
the broad blocks of shadow along the cliff's lee.
My too various eyes could render nothing
of that darkness where scarp met the sea, so nothing
of its melting up warm rock to five battered trees.
Oh, but I got those right, didn't I, those five trees,
and just by little gestures I'd always known were in me.

At Wendell's Garage, Downeast Maine
(Or, The Way Life Should Be)

for Carl Little

So here I'm happily cornered, in the pine-
tree state, from which, at eight, I brought
back my friend Ward's adverb *wicked,*
to sprinkle into my Massachusetts speech
like lupine seed. But even that early stint
at export work won't qualify me as anything
but from-away. Nor should it. From-away-
hood suits me, even after decades here,
maybe since it has made so plain (as maybe
also does living in Mendocino or the Delta
or Ohio) how mediated, not quite to say
caricatured, experience of any place can get.
You know: Homer, Porter, Hopper, Wyeth —
you know, even if you're reading this
in Alberta or Adelaide or Armagh.
Under the wheels of a station wagon
hefted on a big shiny piston, the back wall
windows of Wendell's garage shine.
A xylophone of metric wrenches hangs
beneath the salt-clouded panes, beneath
the lavender horizon of the bay. I pause
over this, not for invidious comparison
with other pictures it evokes, but in mild
wonder at how we live between what's there
to see, and what of it (to make a living)
we've sold or bought or rented or re- and
represented. I've heard it said that only
those who've suffered their hard provenance
have rights to images like this. How then
should one deserve to be at home here, to
try to write and paint its aura authentically?

Imagination is as much about estrangement
as belonging, and surely the realtors would
(just briefly) interrupt, interpose a signature,
a handshake, before the place could start
becoming a part of us and we of it, before
the object of this exchange began to earn
aesthetic dividends. It buys us, doesn't it?
This property in the horizon no one owns.
We all work hard at loving whatever we come
out in the stark summer sun to see or to work:
a blast of spray, lichen-spattered upland
granite, as-yet-un-clearcut pines. Visitors
and natives — at the festivals and parks
you can see us all pay for this: lobstermen's
wives, Michiganders in yachty shirts, crafty,
hippie survivors, big-walleted elders listing
left in their dotage, plump herbalists, New
York acquisitors, and those thin women on
whom you can almost still smell patchouli.
All happily selling each other summer. On our
peninsular vacations I work at perfecting
my wave to them, from atop the steering wheel:
a high sign, a blessing, acknowledging what's
local, lucky, perfect in the bright August air.
But now here at Wendell's that's my car up
the lift, a tie-rod shot, and Wendell now
gravely on the phone to Belfast, the radio
playing an old song I thought was wicked
good when I was a boy, and there in the back
window the estuary fills with molten silver.

Little Homage

No chickens

Of the so much
most depends,
once the hefted
handles satisfy
the grip, upon
the single-minded
wheel, chanting
its circumference
as melody, as route.
This machine's
only moving
part should never
be oiled. After
the song, prints in
moist earth will
signify, though
when only often
proves *thus.* Look
here. Ceremonial?
Or pioneering foot-
steps? Someone
either followed
or foretold a narrow
path into these
woods that are still
recollecting rain.

Eudaemonics

I didn't want my free gifts,
but I wanted them recited once more
before I hung up and returned
to my chaise. All morning (before
it started trying to sell me back
my thirst) the radio in the curtains
across the street was urging me
to consider His illuminating love.
I pictured Him looming like
a president for life above
the fishing fleet engraved on
some exotic dollar, behind all our
industries and pleasures, to be sought
in place of an essence we will never
perceive, since light itself is belated.
(The free gifts, then, were they
providential evidence?) No. Though I
am one fond of coincidence, that's no
quest for grace or meaningful design —
it's just a hobby. I do not pine
for completion, being by nature
more a finder than a maker of
connections, and I dislike spoiling
miracles with questions about
their authors. Why not simply
celebrate? Even Governor Bradford's
chaste estate included a silver beer bowl
and a beautiful violet cloak... When I lie
back in warm light, content as a lizard,
so much comes back: this morning
a path, which led from a croquet
court into cedars — (that led, for all that,
out of burning cities, famished hills,
ambush crossroads, x-ray chambers,
out of dispossessions fate has so far

given me only to imagine) — through
blueberries and ferns, and then opened
on a cove, fringed with sawgrass,
nearly still, dissolving into mist...
Imagining arrival there (from
several summers back) sudden
and strange as prophecy, is mystery
enough for me, and proof: a small,
pleasant life has devoured me entire.
That is why when I left my towel
to catch the seventh ring, and some
promoter's congratulations, I just
wanted her to tell me once again
the contents of my fortune: an apricot
facial, my tires spin-balanced,
four goldfish, and a pound of nails.

Staircase

for Edwin Honig

I thought to give tonight
to reminiscence, exactingly
developed beneath that
starry skylight. But though

your incidental smiles, letters,
bon mots to the wise still
gleam in memory, I keep
returning to those afternoons

when I sat in failed light
on the stairs to your office.
I believed in offices, in mastery
observed, but was far too

solemn to appreciate your
kindness, your genial ironies.
I'd sit on those stairs, cloaked
in Rilke, Mallarme — a novice,

delighted and afraid. Years
before, I'd shrug into a surplice
in a room behind the chancel,
and wait for a big-featured, big

voiced minister, who'd appear
almost late, robe himself in
one substantiated minute, then
nod at me to open the door

on act one of the sacrament.
Forgive the dissonance
of this image — its shriven heart
is a truth I cannot otherwise

approach. You were never
thus accustomed — I never
knew what you would say.
And I don't recall your desk,

or window. Just the bookish,
reverent waiting on those
stairs before your office, and all
the years since, knowing you

were still hard at it, writing
shadows down toward their
imminence at noon, listening
for lines certain and hilarious

as rain. That's what endures to be
said tonight, gratefully, for it
became my sidelong, but durable
conviction that learning to make

lines, in mischievous hope to set
dancing each word's necessary
freedom, is learning how to live
and to love. All the rest is prose.

Vagrancy

From an American early autumn evening
flung back into tomorrow's afternoon,
I sat a while in the car park, smoking
over a map, then for practice drove west
to a neglected town, where transatlantic
flying boats set down seventy years ago,
and on the silent pier beside their museum,
imagined back the long white scuds of their
landings. No one else otherwise like me
would have come here. So now that no one
could take my peculiar solitude from me,
I set out, drawn by the intuition that my
heart would feel welcome on the grounds
of some enduring verse I first read forty
years ago. Intimation, almost invitation —
I felt bound to honor, no, not answer, honor.
Even knowing the big house was a ruin.
Under steep September sky: sea-gray,
lavender, blue, and quartz, I shouldered
a bag, and set off into the Seven Woods
toward the lough, not expecting swans —
all flown, long flown, as that weary spell
of a poem supposed they would be.
But on those woodland paths I made a loop
of several miles, until I'd walked myself
quite out of the life I'd yesterday begun
to shed in the airport lounge. The pleasure
was guilty, but pleasure it was, piercing
as music I wished never to end, a real
dépaysement, an achieved disappearance,
a belonging more profound for its complete
fictitiousness, and I lay down in these
beneath a lime tree in Lady Gregory's garden,
to sleep a just sleep, as in the cherished
crypt of a page. Invisible, anonymous —

who could I fail now? My sleep was not
my own; who was going to wake me?
Nobody I knew knew where I was, knew
that I was this contented tramp dozing
in September shade in a mildly famous garden.
His hour of sleep would change me,
just enough to make the next weeks happen
not exactly to me, but exactly. I woke
beneath the gaze of six red deer.

After Dinner

And while they talk, these things
come to you, returning, sudden as
the convexities of illusions you
seemed to peer into. Little marvels,
to delight or puzzle or amuse those
with whom you're sharing supper.
Then in the time it takes to pour
a fresh glass of wine, the discussion
veers off, and someone else's anecdote
layers over your withheld remark
that, already fading, leaves you
wondering why it ever appeared —
trivial privacy you'll fidget over,
revise, polish, perhaps as an aid
to sleep, after an hour's navigation
back to your tiny bathroom,
where you will rinse the face they
saw listening, that in the mirror won't
betray what it heard and savors now:
someone's story, too improbable
for invention, of crawling out across
a monastery roof to connect a blind
friend's shortwave antenna.. Talk,
talk, talk - drolleries, and casual
speculation, grave conviction, then
again pure amusement. Even if
cheap — mere syllables of longing
or encouragement — still, how these
impetuous rehearsals foster us.
Listen. How fragile they are, and how
liable, when too clever, to suggest
a stylish shuffle, the racquet's nervy
twirl, and the smooth, compact stroke,
whirled like a signature across the corner
of a check. But in these hours after

dinner we trust that words are more
than currency, we enjoy what we
improvise out of having paid attention —
so carefully, perhaps, as to give
a story back some evening years later
to its teller — a simple, affectionate
gesture just to say someone was listening,
across a complex distance, listening.

Departures

In Memoriam A.N. & R.J.B

Past and future devise their moving target,
now, and torture it with neon smog and headlights
until it discovers a refuge, crawling in my chest.

I will never drive this road again, never cross
this long arc of bridge. Every ladder and tool
and cup and costume jewel, anonymous photos curled

among loose batteries in drawers, fifty years of dust
and documents and deal furniture, a crowd of porcelain
figurines, handknit throws, sixty shoes, bedsteads,

tables, sofas, chairs, appliances my wife's cousins
come to cart away, vanished around a block grown
familiar, that I depart now finally and forever, petals

fallen from the trellis stamped on the car. I drive
that glittering bridge down to nothing behind me,
memory already smudged, and now crawling in my chest.

             *

Hours later, across the Sound and east a hundred miles,
pulled in under the cedars in warm southwest wind,
crickets throbbing away above the surf, I stared out

at the dark house a long time. It did not matter that I
know this too will disappear, this sleeping house I have
always known, whose porches and stairs and windows

the child I was still knows. Key turn and latch lift:
memory's tumblers: lilac shadows on the stoop
envelop me again. Naked, clean, wind-washed in my bed

beside the sea, I rose with lightning to haunt
the rooms, pulled down seven windward windows, safe
inside the storm, then sank into a sleep so detailed

I felt nameless upon waking, improbably returned
from some half-remembered, antipodal, actual life.

*

Two months later I would lie down beside my
dying friend, across a bright October morning's hour,
dozing and waking to watch his morphined hands

above the quilt, going about inscrutable, tender tasks:
twisting knobs, drawing cards, turning pages,
caressing a cat, the shadows of a thousand yellow

leaves pouring silence over us. There was no point
asking what lingered from his slant, swift dreams —
the future's foreclosure had made everything a dream,

and pressed the past into pages of devious calligraphy.
But once he woke to tell me how he'd been looking down
a river from a bridge, far down a wide silken river

filled with anchored freighters just beginning to make
steam. I wish I could tell, he said, what all is lashed
up on their decks under tarps. Before they put to sea.

75

Winter Clock

Now *that,* he was
almost thinking, was
beautiful, wasn't
it? Thrust across
the pearl-sheened
window some
sketchy twigs and
one heavy, black
snow-doubled
branch, and from
it a glossy crow's
oblique chandelle
away: baton arc,
smoke script, fled
pendulum, a second's,
the hour's famously
ordinary signature,
fleeting route, at
the after-fling of
which he couldn't
really call what he
felt wonder, since
it seemed to have
departed the coast
of a rumored island
and have been sailing
most of a lifetime
toward him.

Frankensteins

When mother's thespian cough tears through
The old bedroom's wall, I wake first
Into my sixteen-year-old self, trapped
Once more in this house, in the baffled clench
I was then. Then. And then I'm fifty again,
Mordantly familiar with the sullen light
Suburban woods let filter to the windows,
Remembering: the Herald to be fetched, coffee,
The rote of errands she'll contemplate through
The haze of one more cigarette. All my episodes
And eras shake down neat along an armature
Of habit. I shuffle toward the calcified
Showerhead. And in that deluge think about
The family I monthly leave three hours north
To attend this filial duty, about whom mother
Has only the vaguest passing interest.
She made me to come back, after all,
From wherever, after thirty years, after father's
Death — it turns out they made me to return.
No torches drove me back to this scene
Of my old self-regarding rages, inexpressible
Intuitions, excruciations I now sometimes
Witness thrashing in my sons, as they begin
Shouldering their ways out, away from
The strange museum of their parents' life.
I was made to come back to this: the grand piano
Silent forty years, these murky oils of Adriatic
Harbors, her music-box recitals of girlish
Vanities and triumphs, collecting a bitter dust
I cannot bring myself to clean. Be wise
To this, I tell myself on the drive home,
Wise to what you were. To what your boys
Are. It becomes a kind of prayer — Let me
Find a way to honor mania and torpor,
Clumsiness of mood, even as I'd save these

Beloved creatures from themselves, see them
Through (not out of) all their monstrous joys
And terrors toward the human and humane.
And what debt will I be squaring doing that?
Where is the voice to bless all this and mean it?
Isn't there something the man I'm making
Myself to make these lines could pretend I've
Understood? How unlike me he seems when I
Turn the corner back into my life. The house
Of my reputation just last summer had a fresh
Coat of paint. There it steams now, under
March clouds, toward anchorage under lilac
Leaves and birdsong. Upstairs, in the attic study,
The ragged hole a fist made in the sloping white
Ceiling still gapes beneath a blank sheet of paper.

Make Strange. Be True.

for Kate Barnes

You looked, for a moment, in the dark, as if
at something impending over my shoulder.
Not long after, with a few last words
of grateful admiration, I stepped out under
wet maples and turned toward my door.
And when you had driven many miles
toward the sea, I read the pages you'd given me,
and around the noble measures of their
sorrow felt the stillness of my house reassemble.
And something else, which did not at first,
despite a vaguely bitter lonesomeness, seem
to be the admonishment it was: a feeling
that I had just pretended to live where we had
parked, and had walked home many blocks
in the rain, past a dozing cabby, cats in blue
windows, strangers hidden in a hundred rooms.
For the place she came from there were many words
such as blowing curtains, ash trees, weathervanes, stars.
For the place she went into there are no words.
Different people imagine what they must.
We can only see a little way down into
each others' hearts. There are many words
for what happened, for what remains to skid
and drift in the waters' cold, perpetual over-
swing, and since we would have what must
be lost not lost upon us, we would have words
be deeds, we would hold our own in them,
as in a soulful silver Latin — absolute, not
chaplainesque, not tactical but true, sympathetic
and vertebrate as strings. Look it up, my
mother would say, and learn the root by heart.
I thought of roots as stolid lightning, plunged
into soil that suffered and encouraged
familiar trees, toward each April smoldering

into leaf. For years I have kept my head
down, heart set upon the leaves, working at them,
one by one: stipula, petiole, every blade's tiny
coastline in the air. After them. Gather them.
Redeem every green hour, word by word.
But I have not thus more than coolly
comprehended, not imagined past nostalgic
collusions with detail. I have not learned
the root. *She will not imagine any more*
that they might meet again, you wrote, then
imagined that exact disillusion, made music
of the rage that woke inside a spell.
Different people imagine what they must.
Having again rehearsed the tale of my ship's
arrival and departure, I walked in obscure
but certain shame twenty yards to my door.
And reading your lines, saw I have not
understood these instruments, the contact each
must make with what's been lost, denied,
hidden. Learn the root by heart. Let imagination
apprehend the leaves. Where we are green,
where redeeming is not a question of gathering,
but of exactly, harmonically, holding things apart.

At Sea

In memory of my Father

Four years. Four years I told myself were patience,
a matter of discretion and respect, of waiting to be seized,
or seen through by your undeniable shade — wishing

you might happen to me, though you have, gently: where
once I'd heft a small boy to my hip to see himself, now
in a mist I find myself alone, resembling you. My hand

upon the steering wheel is yours, scaled down. There,
in that photo of your bridge vigil as a young lieutenant,
I've been searching before, before they radioed

your ship about my birth. And hereafter, I listen, in my
voice and inclinations, in your grandsons'. They
knew you as a genial, uneasy stranger, who'd arrive every

Christmas Eve for an hour — coffee, and a sit with them
on the rug, and who, one spring at the tiny local airfield,
took us up to see the county. Four years I have awaited

but not tried to wake your confiscated spirit, who loved
things shipshape, airworthy for all weathers, who prized
layering, harmony, fittedness discovered: mathematics,

music, the camouflage of creatures in their element,
the strange, sun-spun fabric of the world. Wonder
was your sabbath — comic, discreet, affectionate man,

in whom the streak of officer ran so strangely close
beside the boy. I am left now to recognize whatever you'd
have loved. No task. A natural function of the loyalty

(your virtue, and your vice), by which in me you still remain
yourself. Which may explain the four years since I ran
down that hospital wing toward you, as down a foggy pier.

Your daughter had, minutes before, already sung you off to sea.
We struggled Academy and wedding rings from your fingers,
which through my vigil all night before had sometimes stirred

and squeezed my own in the dark. Ah, what could the story
of your own death's hour possibly mean to you now? Four
years it has gently urged me to find a language to reach you,

for you too believed ceremony redeems experience.
God knows the austere little service in the church where you
were married didn't do, nor even the fine, loud party your

sister threw on your next birthday: shipmates, boyhood friends,
family. Nothing the least lugubrious, you'd be glad to know —
stories all day, pure survivals of affection in the seaside house

you loved, and to which, so long ago, you sent me back
in your stead, that then I loved and called my home, for all
our forty years of cordial distance. In that précis of our story,

I must place those years between us, to reveal and account
for these lines' undertow. The look you gave me sometimes
in those last six months might have been calling out to my

remorse in recognition. I know better than to ask forgiveness
of the dead — let this suffice. I recognize the things I know
that you'd have loved. And I'd step away in silence now,

step away so you could hear — surely you're not so long gone
into the elements you could not hear tonight your grandson,
yarning of his two-week offshore sail: the swell, the cold,

the boat, the islands, the wind, the extravagant sun. Listen.
Listen — he speaks with love of things you always loved.

Meteor St.

November 2002

Several of the several score we
saw in a cold quarter hour so
bright they lit the clapboards
of the house like lightning, each
a call upon us for amazed,
confirming cries, passed among
us — there, yes, that one, yes.
After a time standing with my
gaze pitched up in darkness,
I grew unsteady; no patriarchal
oak, leaf-shorn, avidly fingering
the certain stars, catching the fallen.
I had to lean against the house
to watch the last few minutes
worth of wild spears flung down
past the roof, or through that elm
whose reach astonished me now
just eight years past its planting.
And remembered years ago trying
to write with indulgently amused
disdain of observing the fore-
known miracle of an eclipse.
But this morning with so much
of what's left of this life uncertain
or decayed, recalling how dawn
exhaustion like this once seemed
luxurious — coffee, loved ones,
half light — I am glad we knew
to rise, glad for the vault of old stars
through which those blazing tails
came lashing, glad now even
that we will all be gone when next
the planet meets such brilliant rain.

Fiction

after Wallace Stevens

Read late a winter's night. Feel the rooms around,
The rooms within the mind resist the dark.
The fire burns as the novel taught it how.

Summer's sounding bowl may ripen clouds
In the pages you pay out beside the hearth.
Read late this winter night, and the room around,

The rooms within you will gently fill with proud,
Passing voices. Even now, in the cedar's heart
Fire burns as the novel taught it how.

So make each hard scene arrive, as if somehow
Foreknown in the cold, complex kilter of the stars.
Read later into the night, until your room surrounds

A world, where flames unfurl awful flags or drowse
In the furnaces of sinners. Where desires pour
Or crystallize as music taught them how.

Rise, old moon, above the pallor of snow,
Summoning pillars of smoke toward
The stars. Read the dark you've loomed around
Us all. The fire burns as the novel taught it how.

Visibilities

The seal's slick head slides from cold,
polished water like the recollected portion
of a dream, into sunlight. He's alone.
And this old world cove another mirror
I say I miss you into, another in which
to fear the monologue you'll someday
make a deed: our cowardices facing
north to north at last, stubborn as
magnets. Maybe we just never made
enough yearning to export, or maybe
desire naturally dilutes to gentle fondness.
I can almost remember waking to your touch,
but the memory I drift off to most
in all these rented Irish bedrooms
is of when, from ignominious overboard,
I watched the black sloop stagger and luff
and reach and luff toward the harbor-mouth,
you and the boys staring helpless over
the combing at my head among the swells,
bobbing, still comically eye-glassed,
unreachable and drifting further away.
My raging shame was the only flaw
in that force five seascape—not your
elemental fear, which from my wave-washed
vantage seemed to belong to some vital
cruelty life was disclosing to us now.
The flashpoint image not of us,
but of the world as it might decide to preserve
or discard us. The story of our survival
that afternoon doesn't matter. Whenever
it seems we're punishing each other
with loyalty again, I will remember
the strange, comprehensive distance
that included us, and the regret so tart
the tongue might almost have sworn it was joy.

ROBERT FARNSWORTH has published
two collections of poetry with Wesleyan University
Press, *Three Or Four Hills And A Cloud* (1982), and
Honest Water (1989), and for more than twenty-five
years his poems have appeared widely in periodicals
across the U.S., Canada, and the U.K.. For seven
years he edited poetry for the Washington D.C.
quarterly *The American Scholar.* Awarded an NEA
fellowship in poetry in 1990, a PEN Discovery
citation in 2005, and the poet's summer residency
at the Frost Place in Franconia, NH in 2006, he
teaches at Bates College in Lewiston, Maine, where
he lives with his wife and two sons.